Autumn's Children

Ashton Nyte

Autumn's Children
First US Edition
Copyright © 2023 by Ashton Nyte

www.ashtonnyte.com

First published by Intervention Arts in 2023

All rights reserved. No part of this book may be reproduced or transmitted in any form or by any means without written permission from the author.

ISBN: 979-8-9887122-0-6 (Paperback)

Printed in the United States of America
by 48HrBooks (www.48HrBooks.com)

Thoughts (part 1)

And don't you know
Even in the darkness
There is a glow
Underneath the harshness
Oh yes, I know, I know, I know
I know, I know
I'll be home soon

(Icicles)

The last words of the last song on my last solo album return to me frequently. I remember sitting back in my studio once I'd recorded "Icicles" and wondering if I was brave enough to release it. Brave enough to let people know how much I struggled with those particular demons and how weak and broken I often felt.

Waiting For A Voice inhabits a very special place for me. We are not often fortunate enough to experience an encouraging ensemble of "firsts." Especially when the road behind us seems as though it may stretch further than the one ahead. In any event, I think that album and accompanying book ultimately paused on a positive note and allowed me to journey a little further.

Autumn's Children began as a batch of rough acoustic iPhone demos in November of 2021. The pandemic had been raging for what felt like thirty years. Life, concerts, and sanity continued to be rescheduled, and I had released the very electronic album, *This Alchemy*, less than a year after *Waiting For A Voice*, with very little in common with each other.

Following *This Alchemy*, I created a darker acoustic solo album and a couple of new projects and then mercilessly shelved them all, as I no longer trusted my judgement or my ability to operate even moderately heavy machinery.

And then, after completing the first few drafts of *Autumn's Children* and exhausting and annoying family, friends and cats with adjustments and mild hysteria, I impulsively went and recorded a very heavy, guitar-driven album by The Awakening called *The Passage Remains* and released it just before 2022 limped out of the room. I felt like there was unfinished business for that project and hoped the double album would calm my soul and rejuvenate my headspace while we all waited for The Great Plague to officially subside. Yes, my compulsive songwriting disorder and war on sleep were fully caffeinated and in full swing.

In early 2023, work resumed on *Autumn's Children*, and here we are. It is a bit of a departure once again, but so it goes. Most of the thirty-something songs under consideration for this album were indeed born back in November of 2021 and the subsequent months. A handful of songs are older and have been waiting patiently in or near those boxes under the stairs. Practicing their pouty smiles and rolling their eyes as the years similarly rolled by.

So, after that clumsy attempt at paraphrasing the last three years, please let me introduce you to some of my new friends.

The Garden

Open your eyes and see me
Here in the glow of the world
Down where the rivers are dreaming
Out where the prairie unfurls

Sweet nectar colours the morning
The Hyacinth hides all her words
From those who have given the garden
Less than the peace she deserves

It's not easy to walk away
Not the easiest thing
The light of this autumn day
Has let the music back in

Open your eyes and see me
Here where the old fires burn
Where everything waits on your heartbeat
And every breath waits for its turn

Where everything waits on your heartbeat
And every breath waits for its turn

Into The Dream

Forever you
Forever me
Drifting away
Above the burning leaves

The empty sky
Beneath our feet
I take your hand
And step into the dream

Into the dream
Into the dream

Forever you
Forever me
Dancing across
Winter's splintered fields

And all we have
Is all we need
You're holding, you're holding my breath
As we step into the dream

Into the dream
Into the dream

Something Beautiful

And I wonder where she'll be
Taken by the morning light
to that place where nothing changes but the rain

Through the cables and the leaves
Tangled up in everything
and nothing feels the same

She believes in something
She believes in something beautiful
Something I have never seen - Oh why

She believes in something
She believes in something beautiful
Something I have never been

Turn the mirror to the sea
Ocean calls out when we go
But the sky's alive with all we'll never taste

Broken china at her feet
Oh I don't think she'll ever know
How I feel when she calls out my name

She believes in something
She believes in something beautiful
Something I have never seen - Oh why

She believes in something
She believes in something beautiful
Something I have never been
Oh I have never been

She believes in something
She believes in something beautiful
Something I have never been

Rivers Run Black

Where the rivers run black
Seamless as the fire
Hold, hold
And crawl

Where the rivers run black
As sorrow
See them shake
And fall
And fall

Gather up the ghosts along the side
Hear them sigh
(Where the rivers run black)
(Where the rivers run black)

Where the rivers run black
Dreamers seem to tire
Hope, hope
Is gone

Feeling time turn back
In the shadows
The healing is
Undone
Undone

Gather up the ghosts along the side
Hear them sigh

(Where the rivers run black)
Time begins to fall
(Where the rivers run black)
Time begins to fall
(Where the rivers run black)

Horses

Just before I spend another page
On who I used to be
Let me take a breath and brush away
The things I think you've seen
As I bow and turn to leave the stage
I wanted to come clean
I've been visiting a secret place
And now you're here with me

Horses
See the horses
Running free
Horses
See the horses
Running free

A constellation of a thousand names
Rivers and ravines
They glide like melody they shake their manes
Shimmer on the sea
I was born into the stolen age
Of actors and machines
Take the blue pills if you don't behave
And drink 'til you believe

Horses
See the horses
Running free
Horses
See the horses
Running free

Cinnamon

Feel like I can make it out this time
But how much longer
Water underneath the bridge is cold
And getting deeper

It's true
It feels just like
The day before
And the day before that too

I still taste
The cinnamon
And poetry of you

Pour a little more into my glass
And smooth the edges
Lining up the frames of moments passed
Frozen splinters

It's true
It feels just like the day before
In need of something new

But I still taste
The cinnamon
And poetry of you

It's true
It feels just like
The day before
And the day before that too

I still taste
The cinnamon
And poetry of you

Go To Sleep

They stand at the wall with some tar and new feathers
Dressing the truth, trimming our hedges
Feeding the young to the path of the broken
Stoking the fires with gestures they've stolen

So please
Just go to sleep
Oh please, please
Just go to sleep

Cut to the bone with their carnival features
Flooding our rooms - a new breed of creature
Swallow our minds as our dreams are forgotten
The mercy is gone but interest is locked in

So please
Just go to sleep
No need to think now
Oh, just go to sleep

Stumble alone
On a bridge
To where we are from
Make us rich
Make us belong
Make us rich
Make us belong

Oh please
Just go to sleep
No need to think now
Oh, just go to sleep

The Little Ones

Can't you see
The little ones
High above oblivion

Can't you see
The little ones
Far beyond it all

Trapped Inside The World

As the day begins to slow
And I wait for you to come home
From another week away
That's the working life, you always say

But it's hard to be a child
When the neighbourhood keeps changing its face
It's hard to start again
You know it's hard to find your place

It's the seventh school I'm in
And I'm learning to pretend
To care a little less
But I know, I know I still need to impress

I'm the youngest in my class again
Some things are always true
I'm trapped inside the world again
I need you to come through
I'm trapped inside the world again
I need you to come through

When the night begins to slow
When the shadows take their toll
There's a part of me that still waits
For you to come home again

But I remember that you left us here
Daddy, you know I do
But I'm trapped inside the world again
I need you to come through
I'm trapped inside the world again
I need you to come through

Your Story

Tell me
Your story
We can go
Over to that perfect place

Where amber
Lights the water
And the leaves
Fall like memories
Twist and sway
Hey hey

We'll conjure
Up the future
With a spell
To keep the emptiness away

And with every word
You give me
We'll grow stronger
While the autumn breeze
Smiles upon your face
Hey hey
Hey hey

As the clouds slide toward the night
We belong
As the trees stretch in the morning light
We belong
We belong

So tell me
Your story
Take your time
We've got this life

Thoughts (part 2)

I have often contemplated the surreal assembly of emotions associated with completing an album, or any piece of art for that matter. This one is no different. Excitement, nausea, fear, elation, deafening self-doubt, relief, fragility, and another 12 circus-loads full of deviants are living their best lives in my chest and just behind my eyes. But so it goes.

I'm not even sure if I'll write a book this time. I have so many different thoughts to explore and seem to veer between succinct clarity and the vortex of *Oscar The Obtuse And His Magnificent Menagerie of Manic Misdirection*, or something like that. Shifting between the personal and political. The intimate and irreverent. The part-time poet and the full-time dreamer.

- - - - - - -

I think the new album is about life. It's about childhood, growth, dreams, disappointments, delights, love and war and hope and beauty and nature and the relationship between the conscious and subconscious, material and mystical, lucid and lunatic.

It is also about loss, both painful and painfully intentional. The way we can finally choose to lose parts of ourselves to make room for rebirth, redirection, resurrection, re-invention, and true inspiration when alliteration fails.

And all potentially perceived pretension aside, I kept returning to the desire to both break it all down and swim in rivers I'd only ever admired from the safety of a mostly tried and trusted selection of boats.

So I kept pushing myself to focus on the words and how I was singing them. To allow the fragility and beauty (and other flavours) of the subject matter to guide my voice accordingly. To be brave enough to be vulnerable and gentle. To be understated and to allow space. Even if that meant shelving songs I was dearly looking forward to sharing to accommodate a better view of the bigger picture.

And yes, I get in my own way. Who doesn't? But hopefully, I do that a little less frequently this time 'round. In any event, it has been a liberating and terrifying experience. Here's to all that lies ahead.

30

Nathaniel and The Glam Lizards

I open my tired, anaemic, bruised suitcase and repack the contents for the fourth time. A second pair of boots is probably excessive, but flashbacks to last night's dream suggest otherwise. Running through the thorn bushes from the Tiger-Mammoth-Thing in nothing but cycling shorts and glamorous but not particularly protective *Ziggy Stardust* socks (from the official Bowie store, of course) had left its mark on my subconscious, sleep-deprived mind. On second thoughts, maybe a thicker pair of jeans wouldn't be a bad idea. And a net big enough for one of those Tiger-Mammoth-Things.

Perhaps I should reduce my coffee intake. Now the bloody suitcase won't close, and I keep hearing the opening chords to "Ziggy Stardust" in my head. Oh life. Where were the spiders? Indeed. My peripheral vision alerts me to the Uber creeping up the driveway. I grab the suitcase too quickly and limp down the stairs cursing myself for all the physical therapy I've just undone for being so bloody distracted by my recent spate of bizarre dreams and questionable fashion choices.

I'm surprised to see someone sitting in the passenger seat of the Uber. As I approach the ageing minivan, I notice that both front seats are inhabited by grimacing faces who have long since left their golden years behind them. Great, now "Golden Years" is playing in my head. Sleep deprivation and a healthy Bowie obsession are having their way with me today.

"Airport, please," I repeat as I drag the suitcase into the back of the van, driving another nail into the months of physical therapy, as the very elderly husband and wife driving duo observe me from the front row of their vehicle, bickering over who had entered the address in their phone's GPS incorrectly.

- - - - - - -

After a harrowing drive to the airport and the usual dance through security, I'm at the finest and only wine bar the airport has to offer. Yes, it is early, but the Uber Drive Of Doom has given me a renewed reason to celebrate life, or indeed still being alive. The man at the table next to me keeps coughing and clearing his throat, and my paranoia is reignited. I choose health over enjoyment and absorb the glass of Cabernet with three long swallows. Once I can distract the waiter from his heartfelt and admittedly hilarious conversation with someone more attractive than most, I pay and move on to whatever horrors lie ahead.

- - - - - - -

The hotel bed is comfortable enough, and the sound of the rain is gently massaging the day away. It has been years since I've returned to this town, and I'm feeling strangely apprehensive. Sleep descends upon me regardless, and with it, a new three-headed Tiger-Mammoth-Thing and a horde of Glam Lizards. Apparently, Glam Lizards are most common in this dream climate, as the cool, dry air greatly encourages the necessary makeup and feathers to live your best Glam Lizard life.

This time my *Ziggy Stardust* socks are replaced with *Aladdin Sane* socks, "well, they should be on by now," I muse. Nonetheless, I wake after endless scratchy running and take a long bath. The rain is still doing what it can to replicate the *Calm* App, and I start planning the events of the evening.

Unlike the weather in the dreams, New Orleans is creeping toward humidity. Thankfully it is early April, so I can still wear something other than a thong and sunscreen outdoors. So a brightly-coloured jacket and ridiculously tight jeans will cheer me up and probably allow me to walk down Royal to Frenchman without looking too bloody tourist.

- - - - - - -

The venue is full, and the band is fantastic. The buskers outside are even better, and I remind myself to remind others that this is often how life can be. Maybe I'll put it in a book. I reach into the pocket of my ridiculously tight jeans for some cash to tip the band, and that's when I see him.

He is clad in a maroon velvet jacket, dark faux-leather pants, and well-weathered, mostly black work boots. He is leaning against a streetlamp, tapping his cane along to the band of Tom Waits disciples who are neck deep in a sludgy blues celebration, complete with megaphone and a percussionist on spoons and tin cups. You gotta love this place.

Maroon Jacket Man nods in my direction and then closes his eyes again, swaying to the glorious cacophony, clicking the long fingers of his jeweled left hand. His wispy grey hair hangs to his shoulders, like the wisteria hanging from the tree branches above our heads. His hat looks like it was carved from a relatively pleasant nightmare just before things turned nasty. Small silver stars dangle from the edges of the hat, catching the light and giving his look that little something extra.

The band explodes into a version of "Rain Dogs" that would make their owner proud. I turn back to see if Mr. Starry Hat Jacket Man approves, but he is gone.

Everything feels slightly out of focus as I attempt to casually seek out his face in the crowd growing in the street, but he appears to have left, or indeed to have simply dissolved into the night.

"In any other town, this would probably surprise me," I say to nobody in particular.

"There is no place quite like this town," says the voice behind me. I turn around, and his eyes meet mine from beneath their starry rim.

"Nathaniel Silver," he says, switching his cane to his bejeweled hand and extending his right. We shake hands, and before I can introduce myself, we are standing on the banks of the Mississippi. The air feels thicker, like it has ingested more than just jazz and alcohol fumes this evening. I am unable to speak but feel an unexpected calm gently draping its cape over my shoulders.

"You haven't been back in over five years. I hope you've been creating something exceptional for us," he says, with his musical voice, scratchy like an old record. I am still unable to speak but nod a deliberate "yes." "Sometimes the muse can be fickle," he smiles. "Here we have the Quarter, the Garden District, the rivers, the swamps, the music, the magic, and many other things you seek. Sometimes it gets a little cluttered and hidden under the tourists, but it is always here, sweet as the beignets you had with coffee this morning." I stare at him with the same strange sense of awe and comfort I've felt since meeting him.

I notice that we are no longer on the riverbanks but are in one of the older cemeteries, probably St. Louis #1. The moonlight silhouettes the many aboveground graves and mausoleums, and that sense of calm continues to grow. I am thinking about the very first time I visited this cemetery.

It was December, and I was in a leather jacket and a pair of obnoxious boots, as it was my first visit to Nola, and I wanted to fly the goth flag, discomfort be damned.

My love and I had visited a Voodoo Priestess later that day, and the veil felt thinner than it usually does. Certainly thinner than some of the towns I've visited further north. The Priestess knew things about us, and maybe that should have been unsettling, but it too was strangely comforting, much like being here with Nathaniel Silver, the man, the enigma, the spirit of jazz.

And suddenly, I can speak again. "Thank you, Nathaniel," I say, with unexpected tears attempting to reveal themselves. "There is so much noise. All the time. Everywhere. I had honestly forgotten that this was still possible. To stand here with you and feel these feelings. This beautiful cycle. To hear your voice and cricket song and the voices, laughter, and tears of those buried here. To hear leaves shuffle for attention in these ancient trees, to hear the river breathing, the distant cacophony of trumpets, pianos, and people celebrating. To hear the prayers, hopes, and dreams of all who have been and will still be. If only for a moment. What a beautiful gift. Thank you. Thank you so very much."

Nathaniel sits down on the edge of one of the old, somewhat decrepit resting places for the long-deceased. He slowly takes off his hat, and the little stars seem to move like fireflies about him. He says nothing but looks deeply into my eyes, into my very being. And I have no doubt that a beautiful new chapter has been born.

Autumn's Children

The world disrobed before me
Like something no longer burdened
By what or how it was before
Like a wish granted
Yet never wished for
And I could feel
And I could see
Again

And the oldest trees
Were familiar to me
Like the scars on my arms
Like the tears of a friend
And their branches shimmered
In the silver aftermath of rain and dreaming
And we danced together
Like Autumn's children

Dream Merchants

Gathered in the quietest spaces
Nestled between feathers and tears
Personified by personable persuasion
The Dream Merchants shifting their gears

High above Saturn or Sunday
Or closer than fervent despair
With palettes of winter and wonder
The Dream Merchants colour the air

And here we believe in the living
And things we have chosen to taste
I know they are waiting like raindrops
And smile as we exit the race

Brighter than sunshine or beauty
Louder than wisdom or fear
Gathered in the quietest spaces
The Dream Merchants shifting their gears

Thoughts (part 3): Trouble

"If you're lookin' for trouble, you came to the right place." What an opening line. Talk about setting the scene. And in the context of his impact on my life, a more prophetic line simply does not exist. The "place" in question has become a lifelong obsession for me. Music, words, performance, expression, and the many related flavours that captured my five-year-old mind still resonate all these years later.

I was already an Elvis fan, but seeing him perform in his black-leather-clad majesty made me a disciple. And then I heard David Bowie reach out to ground control, and I saw my future expand into art and theatre and a thirst for re-invention. And many have followed. So many heroes and heroines. Too many to mention. And I remain a captive to the quest of connection.

Connecting with others, joining the dots in my life, cloaked in the magical flood of nature, swinging from the neon glow of the city, diving further into the colours of my dreams and memories, assembling wishlists that try to contemplate how limited my wishes are. Trying to stay present in it all, somehow. The glorious interconnectedness of it all. The peace and energy in solitude. The many waves worth succumbing to. The many waves worth swimming against.

And yes, "trouble" it often is. A life and an industry that more often devours dreamers. A world that shivers beneath an old, heavy quilt of despair, hatred, ignorance, self-obsession, injustice, and so much darkness. A world of absolute magnificence and beauty, of hope, courage, and love. So much love. And the greatest of these is love, or so they say. Or so I believe.

And I keep writing songs. And poems and little stories and little snippets of slivers of something. Something that weaves it all together. Something to help me understand. To give me hope and help me keep going. And I hope you feel that too.

When it all gets too much, I can still turn to Kate, Nina, Leonard, or so many others. Or I can drown it out entirely with something much louder and angrier. And while the most important relationships in my life are still my loved ones, the ongoing need for connection remains. Thank you for celebrating that with me.

Undressing Sunlight

He stands
Undressing sunlight
Unfolding scarlet
From the wounds
The words have left
And the hollow of his chest

He stands
Caressing truths
And simple rhymes
Rhymestore novel
Novel ideas and ideology
Mythology

He stands
And tastes the morning fire
Burning
Behind his eyes
And through the ties
That once bound
Him to the place
He must now return to

They're on to us

Not everything is meaningless
Doubting doubt is dangerous
Only if the aim is loss

They're on to us

Suspended

Pizzicatos
And other dirty strings
Ring in the new year
Balancing promises
On well-tailored fears
And sentiments sincere
But tyrants
Still focus
Those very big guns
On that sweet spot
Between the eyes

Three Wishes

"You have three wishes," she says. Her eyes are the colour of dreams long abandoned, and her voice pays homage to the endless cigarettes she seems to smoke.

The room is wallpapered in a style that may have been *en vogue* when people still liked wallpaper. Maybe they still do; I don't always notice those sorts of details.

"There are limitations to what you can wish for, of course. The wishes must be unique to you and your life. No wishing for world peace or such silliness. Must be things unique to you." She drags out the word "unique," adding an extra syllable or two, which makes me think of Alexander Lemtov and totally destroys the mystique of the moment.

But that is often my problem. I always have a song lyric or movie quote available to amuse myself and whoever is within earshot. This works relatively well at parties but not so well when a cloak of mystery is in the early stages of weaving.

"The first wish must be used by the end of this week. The remaining two wishes by the end of the month." I have so many hilarious comebacks just below the surface but decide it best to simply nod and do my best Hollywood stare of intensity, complete with a very deliberate and audible swallow. I can almost hear the director cheering, and the foundation for my acceptance speech swims beyond embryo status.

"And no wishing for more wishes, obviously," she says, adding untold syllables to the final word. Now she's reminding me of Brian Molko's career of dancing syllables; maybe she should change her taste in me-hen too.

"So I go now, and you drink the tea," she says with no sense of irony and gestures to the ornate glass of nuclear-hot liquid on the table, doing its best to melt the awful wallpaper. "Ok, thank you," I reply and quietly wish I was born someone else.

Skye

She crosses herself and leaves the room, determined to make it a good day. The last few weeks had been especially challenging. New job, new apartment, and of course, the end of another relationship.

Relieved that rain would be terrorizing a different town for once, she exits the building without any waterproof clothing for the first time in recent memory. It seems to be a quiet day outside. Well, relatively speaking. It is never truly quiet, but rather the din is less oppressive than usual, like when that metal band finally plays a ballad of sorts in their marathon thrash set.

Speaking of metal bands, she reminds herself to unfollow that band that keeps posting those awful pictures. Years of disappointment have made her so afraid of disappointing others that she's found herself quickly looking away from her Instagram feed rather than potentially offending anyone with an unfollow.

And so it goes for the girl most likely to solve the puzzle of life, or so her high school English teacher had said. Miss Grace was such an inspiration; in her Bohemian beads, flowing, earthy ensembles, and gentle smile, every day offered something new. Guiding the class through the joys of Eliot, Blake, Woolf, Morrison, and even Shakespeare.

Sharing tales of college activism in the sixties and the perils of eighties materialism, despite having a crush on the bassist from Duran Duran, but then who didn't? Miss Grace was the one who first told Skye that she could do anything.

After a lifetime of darkness, abuse, and worse luck than the universal median for exceedingly bad luck, Skye felt seen and heard. Miss Grace had first encouraged her to find her voice and then revealed the words to allow her to start shining.

And shine, she did. Despite the usual high school ugliness, Skye found herself and, eventually, her tribe. A small but genuinely kind group of fellow students that soon felt like family. No, Abby, Evan, and William were family. And for almost two comparatively wonderful years, despite the suffocating sense of shame, Skye believed that she had escaped the curse.

- - - - - - -

On a mountaintop, about three or four hours east of Nashville, Tennessee (depending on who you asked), Gavin Barnes is carving a small statue of a horse. It's a Mustang, but Father will probably call it *another damn pony*. As in, *stop screwing around and stop playing with those damn ponies!*

Old Bitter Barnes, as the locals call him, is a perpetually miserable man. Gavin spends as much time as humanly possible playing with said ponies or dreaming or doing absolutely anything to avoid being at home with the old tyrant. For his thirteenth birthday, Bitter Barnes stole the last of Gavin's inheritance and destroyed his collection of carved horses again. He also gifted Gavin a broken arm for the second time. Apparently, the whiskey made him do it. The meth probably didn't help, either.

And so it goes for the boy whose sister somehow made it out. He doesn't begrudge her for leaving; he knows how dangerous it is for her to return to the glorified shack on the mountain. Her last visit nearly ended in her premature demise, and Gavin had spent two weeks in the hospital after trying to stand up for his big sister. So yeah, he doesn't hold it against her at all; he is just so lonely.

He puts the knife down and runs his delicate fingers over the Mustang. It is a beauty. He names her Hermione and starts to make his way down the side of the mountain.

About six months ago, he found a small cave on the mountainside. The entrance was obscured by some wild brush and still is. It has become his sanctuary and a safe house for his carved horse collection and the letters he writes to Skye when life gets too heavy to simply kick it in the knees, as she used to say.

He moves the brush aside and steps into the coolness of his special place. As the makeshift door sways back behind him, he is convinced that someone is in the cave. He stands absolutely still and holds his breath as tightly as he holds Hermione against his chest.

He begins to hear a rasping sound from the furthest corner and a dull thudding. After three painful minutes, Gavin realizes that all the sounds are coming from his body and slowly brings his heart rate and anxiety levels down to something more sustainable. His eyes adjust to the gloom, and he nervously inspects his "home away from hell," as he calls it.

His selection of carved horses gazes down from the rocky ledge they rest on, untouched by anything but dust and time. His letters are still in the partially crumpled, stained shoebox under the same pile of leaves. And most importantly, Oliver is still sitting on top of the beer crate full of straw and whatever other bedding Gavin has been able to procure.

Oliver spreads his wings as if he is stretching off the morning fatigue. Life is pretty exhausting for an Owl in hiding, but so it goes for this Nocturnal Menace. Gavin is still amazed that Bitter Barnes even knew what nocturnal meant, although he's pretty sure the old bastard said *I'm gonna git that Nocturnim Menace and fry im up for supper!*

Fortunately, the old fool passed out moments later, and Gavin was able to guide Oliver to his new nest. He's still unsure how the owl understood him, but their bond has only grown as the weeks have passed. Gavin is still disturbed by Oliver's appetite for rodents and snakes as he'd prefer as little violence as possible in his already troubled existence, but he had learned about nature's good, bad, and ugly ways when he still went to school.

"How is your day going?" he asks the large Barn Owl. Oliver blinks his eyes the way cats do as a sign of affection. "I'll take that as a not-too-shabby, mister," Gavin giggles and sits on the cave floor.

On some occasions, Oliver has even let Gavin gently pet his head or chest, although today does not seem to be one of those days, despite the big bird's loving gaze. Oliver keeps looking at the boy and darting his head toward his nest.

The boy cautiously approaches and sees the unexpected shimmer of something to the side of the bird's deluxe bed. As his eyes adjust to the low light, the form melds to that of an old pocket watch.

He picks it up and wipes it off on his threadbare Def Leppard T-shirt. He wasn't alive when *Hysteria* was released, but it is one of the three shirts he has, and he thinks "Animal" is a pretty cool song. The watch feels warm in his hand. No, not warm, but a tingling sensation seems to spill from its ornate casing.

- - - - - - -

The rain comes unexpectedly as Skye makes her way back to her apartment. Heavy drops rapidly descend with authority and just a hint of sarcasm.

By the time she is in the building and has climbed the six flights of stairs, she's shaking and has developed an unpleasant cough. She runs into the bathroom, stripping the wet clothes from her shivering body, and turns on the shower as hot as it goes, which is usually lukewarm. Today lukewarm feels wonderful, and Skye is lost in the simple pleasures of indoor plumbing and a life with actual doors and windows.

So many memories, so many lives lived before. She feels the tears and turns her face toward the shower head, and enjoys the warmth for just a little longer.

After the magnificent shower, she dresses in an old sweater and leggings and makes coffee. "I'll probably regret having a third cup so late in the day, but oh well," she says to the empty room. Well, not quite empty.

She is suddenly keenly aware of someone or something in the apartment with her. She puts the mug down and scans her meager accommodations and her even more meager possessions for a moment. All appears to be as it should. But for the small picture frame on the floor next to her bed.

- - - - - - -

Gavin inspects the watch, feeling the tingling sensation growing and trickling along his arms like ants searching for the party. He turns the small wheel at the top of the watch's cracked but handsome face and sees the arms move back. Wasn't it Cher that wanted to turn back time, he giggles to himself.

He suddenly sees a very clear image of a younger Oliver the day he first brought him to the cave. He remembers the box of crayons he wrote his letters with and how Oliver seemed to want to eat them, or maybe he was just smelling them. And then it was more than a vision. Gavin was there with the younger bird, having just fled Bitter Barnes' shack on that cold Thursday evening, with his new friend and a new selection of bruises.

- - - - - - -

Skye picks up the picture frame, which seems to have been placed next to an old box of crayons she must have forgotten about. The frame looks familiar, but the rudimentary pencil sketch of a Barn Owl is not.

She feels a strange sensation across her skin and drops the frame onto her mattress. She leans against her only piece of furniture, a grey wooden dresser she had found on the curb a few blocks from her apartment.

Abby and William had kindly helped her carry it all the way back to her building and up the six flights of stairs. Evan had wanted to help but was so sick with food poisoning that he had spent two days in bed next to a bucket and a jug of water. The poor boy still looks like he has missed six or seven meals.

The dresser creaks beneath her weight, and for a moment, Skye thinks it will crumble and explode, sending a cloud of splinters to tear at the curtains and the posters of Jim Morrison on her walls. Her largest earthly possession, turning on her the way everything seems to do. But the moment passes, and the room is filled with only the sound of the rain and her racing heart.

- - - - - - -

The boy turns the watch wheel again, and the arms of time bend back further, reaching for another memory to embrace. It is his father, leaning over him, with a belt in his hands, with bloodshot eyes, screaming all the bad words he knew.

Gavin quickly turns the wheel again, and it feels like the ants are covering his body. He is outside the shack, looking at the small, hideous cabin with that same mixture of disgust, shame, and disbelief as he has every day of his young life.

The second window isn't broken yet, and the front door doesn't have as many of the trademark boot marks and holes that would discourage even the most determined visitor. He also notices that there is still a green crate of empty beer bottles outside the front door. The same crate that now afforded Oliver many a restorative night's sleep.

- - - - - - -

She kneels beside the picture frame and turns it face up. The paper is still yellowed with age, but the picture has changed.

It is another pencil sketch, this time of the shack in which she spent the most miserable years of her life. The hellhole where she and her brother suffered more abuse than she could imagine surviving. The prison with the world's most despicable warden, dressed in anger, hatred, and ignorance, and all the shades of evil's personal palette. The theme of countless nightmares and the birthplace of The Curse.

She feels a surreal sense of separation from herself as she throws the frame at the apartment floor, with all the strength she has used to try to defend herself and her brother on countless occasions.

The glass shatters as the frame's shape is contorted by the impact of the fall, but there are no glass shards or splinters of wood. Instead, the yellowed paper lies on its back, with that repulsive shack staring up at her wild, tear-filled eyes. The numb sense of separation grows as she picks up the crayons and crouches over the picture.

She chooses the red and yellow crayons and starts colouring flames, bleeding from the cabin like the screams of the past. Flames clawing their way up the walls and into the roof. Smoke, black with various poisons, lunging from the windows and into the whiskey-stained summer sky.

- - - - - - -

Gavin's palms glisten as he clasps the watch so tightly that the second hand seems to reverberate through his body.

He stares at the cabin as the fire's insatiable thirst is rapidly sated. Thick dark grey smoke replaces the red-orange glow as the old shack seeps into the ground it has offended for the last nineteen years.

He steps back from the vision and feels the familiar roughness of the cave wall behind him. Oliver is watching the boy with an expression that is not simply affection but something akin to relief, maybe even understanding, if that is somehow possible.

Gavin closes his eyes as the sensation of crawling ants gives way to something else, something like plunging into an icy stream on a scorching day. The sound of rushing water encourages him to open his eyes, and he does. Hermione the Mustang is in his right hand, just as beautiful as she was this morning. The boat is rocking gently on the river as it drifts about fifty feet from the water's edge.

Skye puts down the horse she's been carving and meets her brother's eyes. From the trees on the riverbank, they can hear the owls and smaller birds celebrating the end of the day.

Thoughts (part 4): Willow

If you know me at all or have given my (dreaded) social media an even cursory glance, you will see that I am a cat person. To be clear, I love all animals, but I live in a house with four cats.

Nearly two years ago, the most perfect baby cat came into our lives. Rose had told me that she'd seen a tiny kitten in our backyard. Our house is in a subdivision, where each home is on an acre, so our backyard flows into the other backyards in a lovely park-like setting. We even have deer, raccoons, squirrels, bunnies, chipmunks, and possums occasionally visiting, despite the subdivision being a mile from our local wine bar and other conveniences.

So, we were concerned about this elusive kitten. Because, firstly, we're talking about a kitten. Secondly, she looked too small to be away from her mommy. And thirdly, we have the threat of potential death by hawk, owl, fox, or car looming for small creatures.

My wife and I were on the lookout. We would think we'd see the baby cat and be out there with flashlights, cat food and optimism. And when that didn't work after a couple of days, Rose suggested a squirrel trap. We agreed we would give it a whirl during daylight hours with very regular checks. More days passed, and we feared the worst.

And then, one glorious Sunday afternoon, we saw an extremely malnourished, bedraggled kitten making her way to the food in the trap. And the cage door closed, and we were there immediately and brought her into the house.

Of course, it was a Sunday, and there was a five-hour waitlist at the vet, so we took her to the only room in the house where we could realistically quarantine her: my music studio. We let her out of the cage, and she ran from corner to corner, looking crazed and terrified, like a feral Renfield, and then sat next to a portrait I have of my dearly departed cat, Kylie. As if we needed any more convincing.

I went next door to run the water for the first of many baths she would need. When I returned to the studio, she was lying in Rose's arms, purring! A feral cat, with three paws through the veil to the other side, no less. So, into the sink she went, and so began our war on fleas and worms and malnutrition and all its evil accomplices.

And every day, she lay on my lap in my studio. I would give her food and medicine and inevitably be cleaning up vomit and worms shortly after that. And so it went. And slowly, her fur started growing back, and the worms stopped appearing, and following the fifth round of medication, we no longer felt like she could leave us at any moment.

And after nearly three months of rehab and studio quarantine with Dad, being monitored and spoken to on the baby cam we had installed, and watching her go from almost lifeless to a playful little angel, she was introduced to her siblings. I'd love to say they immediately welcomed her with open arms, but these are cats we're talking about.

Willow is a unique being, and we have an extraordinary bond. In fact, as I started typing this chapter, she decided it was time to lie on my chest again. I suspect to do a little editing. I should probably wrap this up and will try to resist sharing a few hundred photos of her but will leave you with this thought: People often comment on how Willow won the jackpot when we saved her - a family who still cuts vacations short because we miss her. As cutesy as it may sound, we are delighted she found us. We are better for it. Long may she live and destroy cat houses, play with Jarvis, and edit songs, videos, and stories with me, either on my lap, chest, or studio desk.

And if you ever have the opportunity to save an animal from a shelter or, indeed, the great outdoors, I highly recommend doing so. Our lives are so much brighter for sharing them with these wonderful, beautiful babies.

A Few Old Friends

They gather like Willow's white hairs to every black item of clothing I own. Old friends. You may have met some of them before, but I believe they are worth having another drink with. And if not a drink, at least share a few tears. Of joy or other.

Window

I'm outside
Your window wall
Incomplete
Alone
I believed
When you took my hand
Now your eyes are stone

It's like the end of time
Has swallowed me
I'm deep below the hours
I can't breathe

I'm deceit
And you're so clean
Purest angel glow
Don't you wake
I won't be long
It's just that I can't see

It's like the end of time
Has swallowed me
So deep below the hours
I can't breathe

From the album *Dirt Sense* by Ashton Nyte (2002)

Nothing Like The Rain

It doesn't have to be like this
Down on the floor with your heart
It never felt so meaningless
It's over, the hurting won't stop

It doesn't have to be like this
As time leaves and time wounds the dark
You suffocate the emptiness
It's over

There's nothing like the rain here
To wash away the scars
There's nothing like the rain here
Feel it fall

It doesn't have to be like this
Broken by who you are not
Sorrow leaves you with her kiss
And echoes the words to a song

It doesn't have to be like this
Down on the floor with your past
The suffocating emptiness
Is over

There's nothing like the rain here
To wash away the scars
There's nothing like the rain here

Feel it fall

And like some other tragedy
You drift away in spite of me
And like the words I've never known
I'm shown

There's nothing like the rain here
To wash away the scars
There's nothing like the rain here
Feel it fall

From the album *Tales Of Absolution + Obsoletion*
by The Awakening (2009)

Dressing Like You

I gave you up
Sold you out for nothing
And I want to stop
But this is how the future ends
I fall confused
Desperate to substitute
The need to crawl
This desert is another broken friend
To tie up the ends
A friend
That doesn't mean that much to me at all

I only need you when you're gone
I'll be dressing like you

Well, I tried to stop
Buried in the garden
All my favourite thoughts
Eaten by the earth again
I need to lose
Desperate for silence
Oh, I'll find a muse
In everything and nothing much at all

I only need you when you're gone
I'll keep dressing like you
I only need you when you're gone
But I'll be dressing like you

I gave you up
Sold you out for nothing
And I want to stop
But this is how the future ends again

I only need you when you're gone
I'll keep dressing like you
I only need you when you're gone
But I'll be dressing like you

From the album *Some Kind Of Satellite* by Ashton Nyte (2015)

Solitude

Breathe a little deeper
The dance has only just begun
Try a little harder
Try to run
Try to run

The blue of the horizon
Folded out beneath your feet
You don't need a hammer
If you want to be discreet

Solitude
Solitude

War is not the answer
But they've hurt you so many times
You don't want to surrender
Try to hide
Try to hide

Cold as the chapel
Abandoned by the morning sun
You stand in the corner
And I hear you bang your drum

Solitude
Solitude

From the album *The Passage Remains* by The Awakening (2022)

Zero Down

The headline read: they found him dead
So that's what he's reduced to
A woman was found with a carpet around her chest
She said he had seduced her
A bottle corked and a line of chalk
But the readers prefer cocaine
Its effects are grim, but for a lesser sin
We wouldn't have had the whole page

Zero down
Zero down
Zero down

Rumour suggests that Penthouse Pets
Were his source of inspiration
His ex-wife's quote about his need for rope
Oh, what a stunning revelation
We'll include those bits in his greatest hits
It should be out by winter
And then discover the play he gave us the day
Yes, the very day we signed him

Zero down
Zero down
Zero down
Zero down

So we conclude our report with a satirical short
To parody his passion
How tasteful we are as we crumple the star
Who led us into fashion
And if you turn the page you'll hear the lover enraged
By this defiant homosexual
We'll include those bits in his greatest hits
Just hope it's released on schedule

Zero down
Another Zero down
Zero down
Oh Zero down
Zero down

From the album *This Alchemy* by The Awakening (2021)

Fading

Thought about leaving here
But I realize there's still so much to do
Thought about checking out
But I understand that I own this room

And every other story ends
With casualties and casual sympathy
I've got to stay afloat and smile
But where am I and what is there for me

I'm fading
Just like a man

Thought about leaving here
But I realize that we are something new
Angel keep your hand in mine
It's closing time - the lights will be on soon

I'm fading
Just like a man

From the album *Sinister Swing* by Ashton Nyte (2003)

Thoughts (Part 5) [24 February 2022]

I'm sitting in a delightful cafe in Nolita, New York. Too much coffee is almost enough, and I've just started assembling a few bits and pieces to share along with this new collection of songs, poems, and dreams. It is freezing today, and my Zen-like state is mildly disassembled every time a new seeker of coffee and shelter (and an eclectic playlist) enters the cafe, accompanied by icy air from the grey outdoors.

I will finally see the wonderful, legendary, and exceedingly inspiring Patti Smith live in concert tonight. She will celebrate her belated 75th Birthday at the beautiful Capitol Theatre in Port Chester, a 45-minute train ride from Grand Central Station.

Today is also the day that Russia launched its full-blown assault on Ukraine. It feels surreal to be preparing to celebrate Art as many fear for their lives and the lives of their loved ones. I am in a state of out-of-body disbelief and will have to revisit this as I am able to process it all.

Yesterday was the second anniversary of my Father's passing. Two days before that, Mark Lanegan passed. And our hotel is around the corner from the apartment where our beloved David Bowie shared his life with Iman when they weren't breathing in the expansive beauty of The Catskills 100 miles north of the city.

Life, Art, Death, and Magic and the endless blurred cycle of it all. New York certainly heightens those senses. Whether you're strolling by *Electric Lady Studios* and the many gems of Greenwich Village, or The Lower East Side, or the Theatre District, or countless landmarks which celebrate the pursuit of Art and Immortality, New York glows and pulses with inspiration.

Beat

Dissolute and unimaginably young
Tendrils plucked from complacency hum drum
How the West was hung
Beat your drum
And sing for the unsung

Feast upon tenterhooks
Nooks and books and plans we took
How the house shook
With such dreams afoot
Better learn to cook

Bar fight frenzy festive fury
Neon tattoos for the jury
Who comb their hair with smiles enduring
As I saw a starling
Wake the morning

Messiahs baking bread for sale
To all who've learned to give away
The crimson cloth that keeps the cold at bay
And gives the sun her better rays
To grow us all, again

Beat Poetry for those below the waves

The room was a vast expanse, ripe with the echoes of older dreams and the endless tap-tap-tap-dancing footsteps of doubt and synchronized anxiety. I wasn't dressed for it, and I certainly was not ready.

The orchestra was in the furthest corner. Silhouetted against a series of oversized but beautiful paintings of my deepest fears. Surrealist, to say the least.

And words were scarce, for once. "Thank God, it's an orchestra and not an evening of spoken word," I thought as I tried to focus on the lush yet monochrome strings and ignore that tap-tap-tapping just above me. "Someone get that dancer a hearse," I whispered. I can be rude when the stress is in an overt mood (*oh so shrewd* - sad the rhyming mice and lice, rolling dice to the beat of the timpani). Yeah, it's one of *those* movies.

- - - -

Breathing in shallow gasps, rasping and grasping at straw men and saws.

Bloody hell, this obscurity knows no boundless creativity.

And when did this scene shift out of focus and become the inner monologue of a loon?

Can you even say Loon out loud?

Loon.

To the tune
of the spoon
That makes the medicine go down
And out
About
Face
Off

With these hands

With these hands
I built a home
For my thoughts
And dreams to roam
For the sun
To steal the cold
And empty rooms
Of what was never sold

Song for Her

She calls me softly
As if my name
Were safer between her lips
Than out across this ocean
With the sorrowful waves
And the starlight
Swimming and weaving its way
Through stories
Myth
Legend
And promise

She calls me softly
With gentle affection
So as not to disturb
The dreams of others
Both above
And below the surface
Reflecting her moonlight
And music

She calls me softly
But I always hear her
And we will always be
The siren song
The siren song
The siren song
To those
Who believe

With the sky

Now that the light is fading
Other senses are waking
Let's walk to where the shadows
Seem to hide

I woke with another fever
Armageddon's double feature
Here I go again
Seeing signs

You told me you had found a reason
On the road outside Eden
Taking photographs
Of an imminent decline

Where sometimes an old deceiver
Gains new wings and new believers
Dancing in the dark
Behind the blinds

And the valley
I think the valley
never lies

And the ocean
always dances
with the sky

And the ocean
always dances
with the sky

Autumn

Summer smiled
And slowly
Undressed
Outside my window
Her finest
Fashions
Fashioned a maze
Of beauty
On the garden floor
And I raised a glass
And we sang together
And life felt new

Thoughts (part 6):
Autumn's Children and The Red Suitcase

More than thirty songs were written for this album. This is relatively typical for my process. Left to my own devices, I would probably release an album every few months, but I'm sure many would tire of my little circus, and I'd run the risk of boring everyone to tears, or indeed to earplugs and unsubscribe buttons. So, for now, I'm back to an album a year, in one guise or another. But that may soon change. How's that for a rollercoaster of vaguery and indecision?

Moving along... "Something Beautiful" is the oldest song in this collection. It was written way back in January of 2010 and was originally played and sung in an even higher register, believe it or not. It has kept me company ever since but has never had a group of songs it could call friends until this album started taking shape. A rough, wordless sketch of "Go To Sleep" dates back to around the same time, which is also when the little intro melody for "Horses" was written. But both of those songs only really came into focus in early 2022 when I started actively working on the album. The only other elder darling is "The Garden" - written in 2016 or so and was nearly squeezed onto *Waiting For A Voice*, but I always saw it as the opening song to something new, so here it is.

But omission is a painful thing, even if it often allows the songs (and I) to grow in the interim. I sometimes forget what I've actually shared with the world and what is only a part of my life or the lives of the few family members (usually cats) and friends who have heard it. Our youngest son often asks why he can't find a particular song on streaming services, only to be told that I still have not released it. And I can almost hear him thinking that there are songs of mine out there that he is indifferent to, yet some of his favourites still dwell in hard drive limbo. And then, less than half of my released albums are even on streaming at present. Yes, on one impulsive day, I decided to remove a slew of albums for reasons I can't even get into right now. There were terms like re-issue, remix, re-imagine, and other resurrections floating around. I guess time will tell.

It's the same for music videos. I apologize to those who enjoyed certain videos of mine only to see them vanish for no apparent reason. I will try to make them reappear over the next few months, as soon as I find a wand that chooses me for me.

And back to this album. It is a new chapter, as trite as that sounds. And while it was going to be entirely acoustic, one of my other personalities wanted a more stylistically diverse experience, and now we have "Into The Dream," "Rivers Run Black," and "Secret Love," among others.

Oh, I wanted to share a little more about "Secret Love." While some people may not be familiar with the song, it was initially made famous by Doris Day in 1953, and she sings it beautifully. But that is not the version I first heard.

When I was a child, one of the most exciting occurrences was the introduction of *The Red Suitcase*. For inside its scuffed and faded square exterior lived a collection of 45s or seven-inch singles, as they are also known. If you're unfamiliar, 45s are those "little records" that usually only have one song on each side. Traditionally, the A-side was the radio single, and the

B-side was often there to complement the experience. It featured something from the full-length album (if there was indeed a full-length album) or sometimes a stand-alone oddity.

Countless hours were spent playing record after record on my parents' old portable turntable, which, also predominately red in colour, fitted into *The Red Suitcase*, along with the vinyl gems. I first heard many classic songs this way: "Satisfaction" with "Under-Assistant West Coast Promotion Man" on the flip side, "Hey Jude," with a blistering version of "Revolution" on the B-side, a version of the "I Am A Rock" single with the magnificent "Flowers Never Bend With The Rainfall" bizarrely relegated to the other side, and so on, and so on.

And hidden within this collection of primarily big stars from the US and UK was a single by a South African singer by the name of Gene Rockwell. Gene was of the 60's Rock' n Roll crooner stock and had a few big hits in our home country back in the day. Released in 1965, one of the singles, "Ciao," had a simple but haunting rendition of a magical song called "Secret Love," which I absolutely adored. As a young, perpetually romantic child, "Secret Love" spoke to me and has stayed with me ever since.

Not too long before creating *Waiting For A Voice,* I wanted to record a rendition of the song but couldn't find Gene's version anywhere. Sadly, my parents, who were still back in South Africa at the time, had suffered several robberies, and one of them resulted in *The Red Suitcase* no longer being part of our material world and family lore. That in and of itself was devastating to me, mostly due to the fierce joyful nostalgia associated with that box of alchemy.

So I turned to eBay and found an ex-South African living in the UK selling a copy of the single. I bought it, and it arrived, slightly warped but the same pressing as the one eight-year-old me had played repeatedly in the small town of Wellington when my family lived in the Cape for a few years. And when the needle met the vinyl, I was transported back to those early lovesick years and the exhilaration of the unknown, the way only a child can experience it. And I knew I had to capture that and pay homage to this version of this song specifically.

As it turns out, my rendition inhabits its own space, but I feel it owes more to Gene Rockwell's version and *The Red Suitcase* than to anyone who has sung it before me. I hope my love for the song and the wonderful era of '50s and '60s music and cinema shines through. "Now I shout it from the highest hills"…

The River and The Ocean

Hayley carefully removed the photograph from where she had saved it, between the pages of a worn edition of *Brave New World,* and held it to the light. The faces seemed familiar but also unsettling in a familiar way. Despite the paper succumbing to the faded shame of age, their eyes were still the same deep blue of the ocean behind them. And there was something about the ocean that unsettled her, too.

Now in her early forties, Hayley had often found solace in conjuring up *The Early Days*, usually with a decent Chardonnay. *The Early Days*, when life stretched well into the distance and pain was newer and not the old loathsome appendage she could not sever.

Both faces belonged to women. If you could even make that assumption these days, she thought, and then chastised herself for being too judgmental. People were always telling her she was too judgmental. Or too proud, or too soft, or too clever for her own good, or too something. It was how it had always been. And she could sense that the women, *people*, in the picture were quietly judging her shortcomings. Oh, the irony.

A dog started barking in the distance, somewhere in that world beyond her little house at the end of the river. And it was a strange bark. Almost like the dog was just annoyed with a squirrel who had stolen his favourite chewy toy and then joined a traveling circus as *Squirrel with Squeaky Pig*.

Not that she'd seen squirrels steal toys before, but she was often criticized for having a wild imagination. "Daydreaming your silly little life away," they would say. And they would roll their eyes back like demon-possessed exorcisms-in-training, and she would wish their eyes would get stuck. And they would have to be briskly carried to Urgent Care, where the nurse on duty would take one look at them before sending them off to one of those grey, dilapidated asylums you saw in those movies where medical treatment was just another form of torture. "But it still is," she said to the photograph. And the dog kept barking somewhere on the other side of the river.

- - - - - - -

Angelica and Grace were tired of living in the photograph. Tired of waiting to be seen. Tired of being crushed between the pages of Mr Huxley's now legendary novel. And tired of the music Hayley always listened to. Sad songs. Always sad songs.

Even if the artists had up-tempo, uplifting ditties in their collective catalogues, Hayley was a master at cherry-picking the melancholy songs and casting the rest aside. Dirges about loss, despair, and the passage of time. If either of them had to endure another tortured time metaphor, they promised to find the offending artists and drown them in said river, or choke them in those elusive sands that slipped through their fingers.

But more than anything, Angelica and Grace wanted to escape their faded cage. The ocean was not as blue as their eyes. The sad-song-loving sap was mistaken. Their eyes were the colour of majesty. Of winter and a fire darker than any known in the world Hayley inhabited so miserably. And she would learn. And they would teach her.

- - - - - - -

Mondays were never particularly good days. Hayley suspected that while this was probably true for most people, it was worse for her. Mondays were when the echoes were loudest. And the barking dog seemed to know this. He seemed to revel in the repeated sound of his voice the same way The Edge was obsessed with guitar delay pedals. Only it was significantly more pleasant when The Edge did it.

And he barked, and he barked (the dog, not The Edge), and she was starting to think that she may have to summon a small Demonette to swallow his voice, and suddenly the picture moved. She looked back at it. The ocean, those eyes, those faces. She must have imagined it - the movement, that is. "Probably shouldn't have had all that caffeine, especially on an empty stomach," she said to the picture, nervously bending the stained edges. "Life is hard enough without the bells and whistles," she said, quoting Aunt Cindy, and instantly imagined a stadium full of assorted bells and obnoxiously shiny whistles. What a cacophony. A catnip palace for kindergarten-age aspiring noise mongers, she thought as she set the picture on her favourite table. The one she had built with her Dad when he still visited. And the picture looked less threatening there, with the vase of lilies and empty coffee containers she liked to collect.

- - - - - - -

They had waited and argued and pushed and clawed and punched at each other for hours. Grace was wiping the blood from her lip as Angelica adjusted the torn collar of her blouse.

"If anyone is leaving this place, it will be me," Angelica spat. Grace just stared ahead, marvelling at how completely unsurprised she was by this series of events.

If anyone could lack grace, it was Angelica. Mother had played with words in a similar fashion, and it used to drive Grace mad. Now she merely sighed and wondered why she couldn't taste her bloody lip. She was also acutely aware of the absence of any acute sensation. Or any real sensation other than anger at her raven-haired sibling.

"As soon as I get out, I will burn this photograph," her sister laughed, and her flaming eyes grew darker still.

"Go ahead, bitch," said Grace, "try to set the night on fire." And before the melody line of Ray Manzarek's organ could spring forth in memory, Angelica hit her with a rock, and like a rock, Grace fell into the ocean behind her.

Angelica dropped the rock, turned her back on the waves, and realized she was looking at a vase of lilies on her favourite table. The one she had worked on with Dad when he still visited.

Stream #239 (3:27)

The road is the darkest it's ever been. My legs hurt more than my pride and sense of sanity, but I keep walking. Lightning burns its drama into the trees and clouds, and all is electric. Like it was when I used to play bigger venues. Like it was before the silent years. Before the wine and mediocrity. Before Jennifer and Benjamin and the ensemble of lesser saints. Back when I used to dream in monochrome because it was cool, and I chose to do so. Back when I could close my eyes without thinking about the work I needed to do. I was simply too busy working on the right things. Dreaming essential dreams. Playing essential roles in the ever-cascading script that I never really needed to commit to paper, or the cloud, or whatever. But now things are different. People don't wait until intermission. They speak about traffic and food and pop stars with chiseled abs and excavated brains. They speak about posting and post about eating and eat with their mouths stuffed with self-importance. And the art is no longer important. And I had to turn to darker things that are no longer dark in appearance, thus making it more difficult for those who had once loved me. And I no longer love me in that way. But I sometimes think that is healthy. Like running on empty or smashing your favourite guitar, or burning down your favourite room in your house, as long as your cats are safe. But sometimes I think that's just the wine talking. Like the way I talk when the wine is working on the screenplay. The one that never makes it off the cutting room floor. The one I step over and sometimes slip on when traversing the cutting room floor. Fuck that place. Why must everything be so perfect in my limited understanding? Why do birds sing? Indeed. Is harsh language really necessary, or is this stream stronger than the last? Should I swim naked? Should I take the stream and run along its banks until my feet bleed and a new stream is strung where the clouds once hung, simply undone? Oh, rhyme, rhyme, rhyme, always bloody rhyming. New Messiah of the Week. Flavour of the Weak. Scream before you speak. Turn your brother's cheek. Is this what you seek? I wrote a song years ago called "Fascination." Maybe that will get them. Who are they anyway? And will they find me? Here on this road. The darkest it has ever been. Nah, it's been a lot darker, friend.

Thoughts (Part 7)

There is probably more to writing a book than this. Balancing on this web, like I own the place.

My sister and I were woefully uncool as children. One of our most beloved VHS tapes was not an arty exploration of edgy expressionism but a South African theatrical musical of *The Rime of The Ancient Mariner*, captured on video, complete with cheap props, over-acting, and that brightly lit sheen local television often has. To this day, I can still recite Albatross-inspired lines from the play.

Thankfully we balanced that out with endless selections of music videos initially recorded from our limited TV music shows by my father, whose passionate love for music was infectious, and I'm still infected.

From the earliest eclectic compilations of Eurythmics, Duran Duran, A-ha, INXS, Billy Idol, Tina Turner, Madness, Queen, Bowie, Kate Bush, U2, and Springsteen to retrospectively discovering all the '60s and '70s had to offer, a solid foundation was established and frequently repainted.

I loved seeing early footage of the Beatles and Stones, building on my Elvis love and making me certain that everything that happened in black and white was just cooler than the technicolour '80s and over-saturated '90s. But I loved it all and still do. If it speaks to me, I'll keep listening.

When I was 13, I was hit by a car while crossing a road on my bicycle. The driver was speeding and took a blind corner into me. If he'd hit me a split-second sooner, I would have lost my legs. As it was, I ended up with a badly broken arm, head injuries, and a selection of broken-glass scars on my arms and face that have given people twice my size pause in a potential bar fight scenario. A small silver lining, I suppose, especially for someone who has to force-feed himself to weigh more than 150 pounds.

I won't go into details as Rose hates hearing my many tales of near-death events and other medical adventures. Suffice it to say, I've done my time with stitches, plaster casts, biopsies, and all of those delightful tests and scans that leave you feeling grateful to be alive outside of a medical facility.

The other positive is that for many years, I was pretty convinced that I must be here for a reason. Somehow, I've been miraculously spared many, many times, and the very least I can do is be grateful and make an effort to celebrate life in all of its dirty imperfections.

Yet, I lose sight of that. I struggle to remain positive, and I succumb to depression and his myriad of friends more often than I'd like to admit. And it runs in my family. Along with a range of less-than-ideal traits and disorders and every day is a unique challenge. And every day is a blessing. It's just not always easy to choose the appropriate truth for the situation you find yourself in. For some reason, I, too, raise the bow and shoot the bloody albatross over and over again.

But as I write today, the glass is half full, albeit of a wine that may not be the blend I was hoping for. Half full, nonetheless. Hell, more than half full. It runneth over, and there is never a dull moment.

The River

The River
Unfolded its voice
And ambitions
Across the thirsty valley

I stood
A fair distance from its shore
But heard its songs
As clearly
As though I was drifting
In its cool embrace
The way it used to be

Sparkle Kid

Powdered hands
Sweating lights
The breeze
Becomes a storm
Motion born
In a village
Far from where he now flies
And perches
And leaps
And swings
With unfettered ease
It's just the Sparkle Kid
And his trapeze

A vision in blur
Blurred sighs
Blurred heights
So many nights
Tightly wound
In his newfound freedom
To shimmer
And simmer
The hearts
Quiver
In unease
It's just the Sparkle Kid
And his trapeze

Every page
Another stage
Another sage
Wise
Beyond his tears
Above the gears
The engine sparks
But never steers
His world
His dreams
His need for release
It's just the Sparkle Kid
And his trapeze

Firsts

Kiss - Mandy, on the carpet at reading time. She was six, and I was five. I wasn't expecting her smiling, semi-toothless kiss, but for a boy who would eventually be voted third ugliest in his high school class, this was one of the better days.

Stitches - At pre-school. I was four, and some genius threw a wooden brick into the air, and as Bono once sang, "Throw a rock in the air, you'll hit someone guilty." Although my list of sins was pretty short at that age.

Celebrity Crush -
Male: Michael Hutchence (obviously).
Female: Susanna Hoffs (just as obvious, really).

Girlfriend - Victoria. I was nine, and she was ten and a little taller and wiser than me. She was lovely. We were friends at school, partly because she was lovely and partly because there were only seven children in our class at the time. We were all friends. Victoria and I went camping with her parents in the mountains one weekend, which was pre-teen heaven. It was also where we pledged our undying love for each other, come what may. And then, my parents decided to move again, and my world was uprooted once more. As my song goes, "It's the seventh school I'm in, and I'm learning to pretend."

Acoustic guitar - I don't remember the make, but it was an unappealing light brown, challenging to play, and belonged to my girlfriend's brother. Growing up where and when I did, meant not having access to things like guitars until my mid-teens. I taught myself some basic chords but started writing acapella songs in my early teens. Once I could play even a single rudimentary chord, my songwriting catalogue exploded. Once I could stitch together four chords, the world was my musical oyster. I ended up plugging the guitar into a rusty, yellow Boss distortion pedal (horrific tone be damned) and writing some of the first Awakening songs. "Past Idol" and "Focus" were written and performed live while I was still in my first band, Martyr's Image, but more about that if I ever write a memoir.

Electric guitar - A black Washburn with a floating bridge and whammy bar. I wanted a black electric guitar, and it was the only black second-hand electric in Uri's *Music Connection* (original location) in Johannesburg (1995), which expedited the decision-making process significantly. I played that guitar at every show and on every album until my first Schecter, which I got some time after recording Razors Burn (2006).

Concert (The Awakening) - *The Fridge* at The Gasworks in Johannesburg in February 1996 at what was billed as a Gothic / Industrial rave. The Awakening went on first, followed by elder statesmen Battery 9. Jenni's bass was unplugged for the first half of the opening song, and my microphone died halfway through the second song, sending me running off the stage to grab a backup mic. It was still absolutely fantastic, despite my questionable fashion choices.

Concert (solo) - Launching *The Slender Nudes* at The Victory Theatre in Johannesburg, May 2000. The theatre had recently hosted both *The Rocky Horror Picture Show* and *The Jim Rose Circus*, so I thought it would work out just fine, but it ended up being spectacular. We incorporated a hair and fashion show and had the videos for "Glam Vamp Baby" and "Need For Air" on the big screen between set and costume changes. I even have some video footage of the event in glorious grainy super-low resolution. I'm saving it for the 25-year anniversary release, along with clippings of the ridiculous amount of press I got for the album and other bits and pieces. Had I known I simply needed to introduce colour to my wardrobe, I would have done it sooner. Yet, I still shelved the whole project and pivoted back to The Awakening with *The Fourth Seal Of Zeen* in November of the same year (barely six months later). If I didn't know better, I'd suspect copious amounts of cocaine. The truth is too much caffeine, an addiction to creating new work, and the ridiculous impatience of youth.

Theatre performance - *The Slender Nudes Cabaret* at Die Teaterhuisie in Pretoria, May 2001. I'd written a little theatre piece around the album and performed it with two of my *Slender Nudes* friends and bandmates: Kate Towsey on bass and Frankie Clark on keyboards. We did a four-night run with my dear friend Matthew Fink on sound and lights, and it was magical. I met some future friends at one of the shows, leading to my second theatre appearance at the *National Arts Festival* in Grahamstown, but that's another fabulous story.

Festival - Headlining the second stage at the Oppikoppi Festival in Northam, South Africa, with The Awakening in 1998. We had only been touring for a couple of years, so it was a pretty monumental occasion to be playing to around ten thousand people. And there we were, three boys with too much eyeliner and a drum machine, on an unseasonably sweaty and very dusty night in August. We started with "To Give," and I soon realized the perils of running the entire length of a real festival stage before the song had ended. Breathless, sticky, and delighted to be there.

Song on the radio - The demo of "Past Idol" was the first song of mine I ever heard on the radio in early 1997. National alternative radio guru Barney Simon was given the demo by Leon Erasmus, who was producing *Risen* with me (very slowly, as I could afford the studio time). Sadly, Leon failed to label the demo, so it was a bit of a bittersweet experience as Barney praised the song but thought it was by another band. It's amazing how significant that felt at the time. In any event, the record was set straight, and the song got a good few more spins before *Risen* dropped, and the focus shifted to "The Sound Of Silence," which became a rather unlikely hit for a little band that was a complete anomaly at the time.

International Tour - In 2004 we left the sunny shores of South Africa for The Awakening's first US tour. Despite playing to fewer people on the entire tour than we had at any given show in South Africa at the time and driving obscene distances through parts of a country that hadn't yet fully accepted sushi or gluten-free dietary restrictions, I loved it. It was certainly humbling and strangely inspiring.

Book - *Waiting For A Voice* (2020). I was finishing the album and was struck by how the words looked on the page, so to speak. My writing had become a lot more personal, and my brilliant, patient wife had been urging me to release something other than music for years. And then my Dad died, and Covid started a couple of weeks later, and the writing seemed to help. It always has, but sometimes we need a rather significant catalyst, it seems. In any event, I am proud of that little book, mostly for actually doing it. That and my *Ghostboy* character may need a reprise at some stage.

The Awakening's first live concert, at *The Fridge* at The Gasworks in Johannesburg, South Africa, on 17 February 1996.
Photo by Jacques Booyens.

Numbers

I stood at the altar. The altar stood on a floor that looked older than time. And time stood still.
One by one, the doves gathered above. Gazing down from rafters and falling stars. Gazing down like memories, lost in rainfall.
And two by two, my dreams were revealed. To sleep is but to dream, they say. But sometimes, I just dream of sleeping.
And by the third hour, I was hungry. An ache in my empty stomach. A yearning for direction.
And the room was in four equal quarters. As reflected in a sketch above the mantle. Drawn and quartered.
And on the fifth day, I wept. For I was squandering the gift. And I still needed direction.
And six evokes devils. But none of the devils I know care much for the limitations of numbers.
But where are we going with this? Seven sons? Seven trumpets? Is this some sort of biblical thing?
- Only if you want it to be. Let it be. Let it be me.
So now you're quoting songs?
- Aren't we all?

Unto Self

"Here," said the voice beside me
 And conjured a sorrowful verse
Dressed in ink and agitation
Alluding to something worse

"Now," said the childish abandon
And motioned toward the fire
Unwittingly casting a shadow
Subconsciously stoking a trial

"Again," said the sparks on the mirror
Surrounding the places I hid
The thoughts I had carefully assembled
To bury the lines on the grid

"Stop," I swear I can hear it
Like broken glass on the floor
I'm turning and turning and turning
And twisting the rules of the war

Autumn's Children (a fragment)

Autumn's children
circle the edges
step back from their ledges
and breathe again

Autumn's children
Loosen their dreams
From Machiavellian streams
where all is forgotten
and how it once seemed
is ill-conceived
But seldom loses its sheen

And the beat goes on
Beyond the machine

Sometimes Piano

The music seeped through the ceiling and dripped onto her pillow. She didn't mind. Despite the quality of the playing and some dubious song choices, she loved hearing her mother play. It always reminded her of their family home in Cape Town. Well, not quite Cape Town but the small seaside town with its colourful imperfections and the little house behind the petrol station, where she had spent three idyllic years. Before the floods and before Samantha Van Der Berg and before Guns 'n Roses had released "Patience" and how she needed a little more of that these days.

In those wonderful *Before Times*, Jess could ride her bike up and down the neighbouring farm roads. Stepping back hard on those *back-pedal brakes*, or whatever they were called, and skidding for at least three hundred metres at a time. She'd never measured, but it was at least that far, or so Jason had said.

And now she's thinking about Jason. The skinny British boy with his super cool parents who were the talk of the community for the better part of six months. His dad, with his spiky black hair, well-groomed beard, floor-length leather coat, and an earring - oh, the scandal! And his mom, in those very short shorts and hair Jess had heard her aunt call *Peroxide Blonde*. Whatever that meant, it looked super cool. And they were super cool, even though Jason was so very thin and always looked tired, or so Aunt Megan always said.

And now Mom is playing the theme song from that old TV show. The one with the three old ladies and the even older granny, who apparently was the youngest of them all in real life. And the oldest granny, Sophia was her name, put on her Walkman headphones in that one episode and started singing "Purple Rain," and Mom and Dad laughed, so Jess laughed too. But when she asked about "Purple Rain," she was told she was too young to watch it, and that's how it always seemed to be. Living just on the outside. Never quite getting the joke. Never being the first to be chosen for any of the sports teams. Well, to be honest, usually being the last to be chosen, but apparently, that builds character. At age nine, her character must have been rock solid. Or titanium-solid, like Terminator, which she was also too young to see. But she laughed nonetheless every time Dad said, "I'll be back" in that weird voice.

And the sound upstairs is becoming more distant, but she can still identify the song as something from *The Wall*. It was another movie she had been too young to see but had watched repeatedly in her teens. The well-worn VHS copy revealed the gaunt browless man asking if there was anybody out there. She had often wondered the same thing. She, too, had often become comfortably numb. She didn't need no education but was dragged from one small-town school to the next. From one almost group of friends or strangers or assailants to the next. Plucked from one tiny, well-fought-for, seemingly elusive pocket of solace to another place to start at another starting line. And eventually, she stopped trying out for the teams. And eventually, she stopped trying. And eventually, she stopped believing. But she found her way back.

"Girls Just Want To Have Fun" is a radical mood shifter, especially as Mom always chose the reggae reinvention to warm the room when things just got too cold and smiling wasn't as easy as it used to be. But Jess is smiling now. And the light in the bedroom feels different. It may be time for brunch and maybe a cup of tea; she thinks and stretches in front of the closet. She chooses a pair of black leggings and an oversized INXS t-shirt, perfect for Saturday morning relaxation, and heads upstairs.

Jason is sitting next to the tape cassette deck as Mom's piano soundtrack ends in the key of F.
"Thank you for playing that today, my darling," she smiles as her vision blurs ever so slightly.
"Of course, Jess. Maybe we'll head over to the park today if you're feeling up to it?" he says with poorly disguised apprehension.
"I actually think I'm ready to drive further up the coast today, Jason. She's not in that little box. She is everywhere. I think it's time we returned her to the ocean, as she always

wanted. All those years up in Joburg, all that time spent waiting to live again. Waiting to live here again."

"If you're ready, I'll pack the car, and we can make a day of it. Maybe stop at that wine bar afterwards," says her husband.

"That would be lovely. They always have a pianist playing there on Saturday afternoons," she says, wiping her eyes with the back of her hand. "Just bring Mom's tape with for the car ride. I think we could listen to it one more time on the way back," she smiles and gently squeezes his hand.

About the Author

Ashton Nyte is best known in the magical world of music. He is a singer, songwriter, multi-instrumentalist, and producer. At the time of this publication, he has released eight solo albums, eleven albums as The Awakening, one as Ashton Nyte & The Accused, and has lent his vocal, lyrical, and songwriting abilities to several other projects. He was born in Port Elizabeth, South Africa, and relocated to the USA in December 2007. He lives with his wife, mother, son, and an ever-growing ensemble of rescue cats in Upstate New York and Saint Louis, Missouri, USA.

Music Releases

Ashton Nyte
The Slender Nudes (2000)
Dirt Sense (2002)
Sinister Swing (2003)
The Valley (2010)
Moederland (2014)
Some Kind Of Satellite (2015)
Waiting For A Voice (2020)
Autumn's Children (2023)

Ashton Nyte & The Accused
Headspace (2005)

The Awakening
Risen (1997)
Request (1998)
Ethereal Menace (1999)
The Fourth Seal Of Zeen (2000)
The Fountain EP (2001)
Roadside Heretics (2002)
Darker Than Silence (2004)
Razors Burn (2006)
Tales Of Absolution + Obsoletion (2009)
Chasm (2018)
This Alchemy (2021)
The Passage Remains (2022)

Bibliography

Waiting For A Voice (2020)
Autumn's Children (2023)

Gratitude

Jesus Christ, Rose, Tristan, Julian, Becca, Mom, Dad, Candice, Carl, Ryan, Tina Benitez-Eves, Damin Smit, Michael Ciravolo + Schecter Guitars, Kip Kouri + Tell All Your Friends PR, Matthew, Sarah, Ava + Felicity MacEwan, Terry Pirrong, Bob + Jan Kraemer, Matthew Fink, Anabel DFlux, Tyler Bates, Todd Davis, Tish Ciravolo, Michael Rozon, Wayne Hussey, Grant + Jayme Muench, John + Judy Ermold, Jonty Langley, Margaux Crump + Jake Eshelman, Erika Blumenfeld, Donnie + Shane, Randy + Debra Cole, Steve + Tony, Cheryl Keil, Eamonn + Drucilla Wall, Kerry-Ann Allerston, Kari Kimmel + Glow Music, Agata + Christopher Williams, Eva Lhum, Curt Landes, Dave + Michelle Thompson, Mark Lee, Judy Lyon + Torched Music, Dirk Aukthun

. . .

All photographs by Ashton Nyte unless otherwise noted.

www.ashtonnyte.com